Keisha Ann Jacquet

Keisha Jacquet

BY

KEE-KEEDY

To order additional copies of this book, contact:
Xlibris
1-888-795-4274
www.Xlibris.com
Orders@Xlibris.com

Contents

CHAPTER: KEISHA FATHER STORY

I have respects and love for everybody in this world on earth. I will keep in touch with you Christ have respects for the world in A earth some friend or enemies don't like Christ world. We have to level this outsides world out sides earth.

Paragraph: Cast out enemies) Keisha cast out enemies keedy vers enemies keedy destroy enemies. Keisha Betrayed her enemies Kee-Keedy war Battles enemies) Kee-Keedy fright against Battles. Keisha verse family friend enemies.

Sentence: who is Keisha? What are Keisha? were did it take place? Why Keisha is her? when did she now about Keisha? I have a peace Joyed in myself. My life A peace mind Body A peace soul, Soul Sold. She peace Queen soul a peace mind body money in home.

Topic: 1 the Blue sky it from heaven A Blue cloud from heaven A Blue Around the earth can from god the Blue sky is real on this world in the true some rain is a Blessing going in out in the field the rain like Blue or gray Keep trouble a around you wow it Bad Because she have put it a ways.

Topic: 2 A Blue sky is come from lord who creates heaven in the earth the lord Creates heaven in the earth Blue fold to go to school in the Back package At college A Blue sky it tell the true like blue is wash my sin with all my. I wash a ways my sinful that worryful problem around me that Doing things right now.

Topic: 3 they have a blue bowl there have is right now some are them have dishes Bowl Blue sky make the light come out on a Claude Blue from water open likes Ocean Moses in David Blue water wash away from sin .Keisha have Big Heart 101000 wash away problem somebody playing Jokes on me with this games called Kiddie race games.

Index: 1 A flowers is a plants like a green or red flower the green grass go around like a shape balls the green flower is a money problem there have a green Prayer cloth to praise on me A flower is green plants likes in tree the prophet of the Bibles the light are the world sun shine.

Index: 2 some flower grow in the trees some enemies will be empty hand for good. Keisha take her life for grants with these people out her some person have take picture of me in but in the Bowl insides the place I take my life grants good. It not A Jokes around me to much they have problem Index solve I'm is ashamed of him.

Index: 3 the insides a green flowers is red yellow and green it all so good on the earth Dop you know what flower come from A dram) job in John with the prophets word the green flowers some way come in the next days there or spirit of green money wallets. In pure in the pockets by pay your titles in office make a vow to the lord in he want turn Back in first fruit office A green flowers is grow around the world that on the Grass.

Paragraph: 1 the sun is shine a sun is shine a sun is real the sun true A sun is light it come out in the morning ever evening in the Darkness at night come out in dark Black people come out sides at night he or she have so much evil insides them right now my enemies Be fallen against me I have a result on me right now from going down the send he is worryful be praise from raise up the sun going down the sand he were to Be praise.

Paragraph: 2 what go up much come down be fallen Back on you I love you very much in you love me to. I have Baby Dad around me ever my Brother or I love very much Be I stayed prayers for then them ever wants I go out and come in right now I be care who walking me in not no Blood family.

Paragraph: 3 what is raise, rise Arosa against Keisha will flee a 7 ways 8 times Defeat around you. They will be gone off Keisha mind, body, and money off for good they not come back at all for 5 years ago the fright to much I can take no more what no more.

The father is Leonard he was born in July 7, 1936 he stayed in the prepark street he was working at New Orleans Louisiana 70117. He working at New Orleans police he gets along with boys in girl together. Keisha dad is Nelly Bornmen Claydia also joseph Richard Jones is Jackie best friend at Brooket T Washington high school Nelly Bornmen Claydia. I know what is best for him. Jackie dad names is LLoyed Jacquet SR. LLoyed Sr. Jacquet have a high school he was fight against the world war for American.

Bathroom like bubbles in the with candle around it like saw music RB song rose in the Bed room bubbles bath turn off the light candle with black eye balls you can hard see girl what kind of blood run in your body is Aids blood are clean blood you can tell clean person like a spirit at noon day they called spirit around here body in spread in red blood they called hiv that not lord blood at all.

Rose is red violet or blue I love you like the cloud are blue the yellow flower green like money protection with gold brown is house red is a spirit man only I stay in church . I will have me a lord man in my life. A boys make your life short in up bad attitudes make worry chose I feeling weakness because not have a on me.

Is the looked face pretty body or the clothes line supposed you have bad drams would it come true yes or no my answer it will come true if you let it come true better it all ways come false dreams not reach I know what people stand up against me what is the hatin or love that my person being dead I feeling play because the person raise up on don't fear me at all.

Of those who a rosa me can never fall back on them self so why you on don't fear me at all. of those who a rose me can never fall back on them self so why you fall a back against yourself just being afraid what there are they got hand to looked up on.

Sentence: the sun shine A green flowers she have a Brown house A grass is green on the ground in the world and earth reading A Bibles is real faith come true the light of world. I will read is the Bibles telling me so Bibles is reading is better for you. The Lord god in Jesus Christ is on the cross for the Bible.

He will care my blood in my vein with me at all time ever went they asked or presence for seem he will run in my read Blood going in or out my past at all time ever went there presence he lost a lot of hope in Dreams giving up some body true love very much have to said Good Bye very soon I tried to have a good life somebody all ways tired to stop it that American history or a salves movie Do you have A history with the teacher of yourself they. Tied shot a person with false states with Rhyme word about riddle same as games a men supposed to like candle in the Bed room in Make out a Romans looking eye to.

4 Bacterica—Metronaidazol 2 Bladder—Azithromyah No STD Negative gone done end No HIV, No HPV

Nosugar Diabates no high Blood pressure no brain tubes no brain disorder Uterus Clear Rectum clear no bladder infection low Blood pressure Iron Vision Clear no without condom Latex P no none Rubbers no Vignal Medicaid or Medicare A,B,C, in D keep in touch 33 years old 1985-2015 thanks you 300 million professional people Linkied underwritten sickness under Law sickness under mistake sickness Back lie enemies Back lie line under jokes underwritten jokes under law jokes under mistake jokes.

KEISHA UNDER LAW BOOK STORY

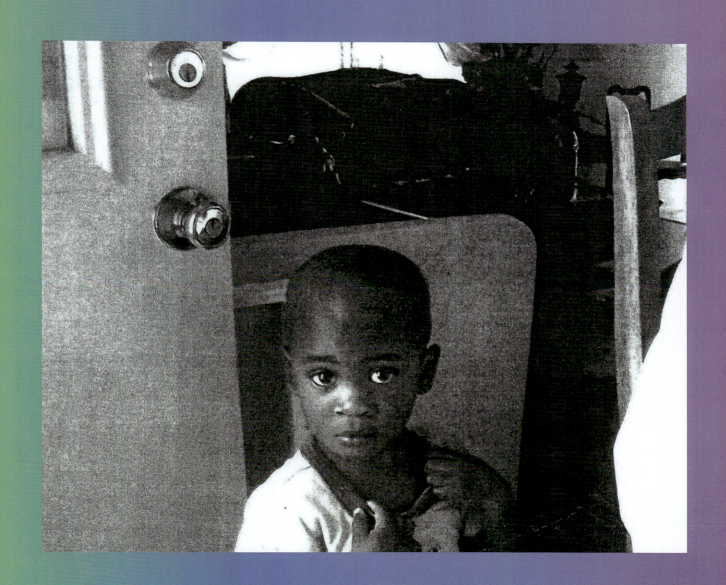

Under written evil done under law evil done, underwritten under law gray law gray stone underwritten law black law black law WXZ little young boys died, dies row gone born done born end born enemies born dies born dies row sos charge enemies died born died row sos sentence enemies Wxz born end gray born end evil enemies destroy weak destroy evil gone done foolish

Hey mother hey baby mother home who for me Keisha Baby mother home hey baby mother Keisha home bust it baby mom called you all A way us home Keisha. Keisha Horizon put it on ya Keisha fire or love desire of your heart.

20 Keisha nationwide out sides 20 Keisha world wide in sides 20 6 pack 20 8 pack 20 professional private action 20 mocking 20 professional 20 action war 20 action law suit 20 action Keisha 20 fiction code 20 non—fiction code 10 black 1000 or million 20 green 20 hero Christ heritance 1 0 billlion 9 pian inheritance evil out heritance evil out sides heritance haven earth color rainbow earth pi an bright earth plan world earth plan Mars plan CIA code gov Washington code gov CIA police station in mate in made in male action Christ in mule in mute sight done gone end sight end sight dies row died row X-woman X -girl w—woman w—girl Z-woman Z-girl WXZ boys WXZ girl codeS-woman S-girl 0-woman a-girls-boys s-man A-woman a-girl b-woman b-girl c-woman c-girl ABC boys ABC girl 20 Keisha like me 20 insides Keisha 20 out sides Keisha in me 20 keisha like you this story Base on a true story beginning to the end story keisha make history story on 9 earth ball A pain a round is chose I know my story right I'm is a no mistake person I'm is a big mistake then she have strong feeling A Heavy Load soul heavy load sole I have heavy heart is red blood I'm is you yoke destroy evil !Illness I'm good health blue sea green sea yellow sea red sea white merry white weeding Keisha proper names proper word proper number Keisha proper private policy white trust in have faith far tale you push me hard he try one way trust in have love Queen Cinderella Queen super star most very like it magic ball magic show rose is red violet or blue magic card in magic show for you will be my fairytale like Keisha Barbie Doll Rose is red violet or blue I love you Do you Loving me.

Hello my name is Keisha Ann Jacquet better known as kee-keedy@ 2015—2016 I'm is A Honest homeless person one hurricane katrina 2005 I'm is generational girl was a salves person in my home market like stand home that was not fix right on pre park I'm is a homeless girl generational salves people civil right war 1942—1965 my dady told my undo step my on a skills on the floor in he weight me and see how much I work for myself over 1,000,000 salves girl Keisha 19982-1983 new born girl with light on me for my sides head that why Jesus walking insides me right now on my head it was on a wall.

Sick In the head sickness, In A head sickness in A Brain tubes pay ILLness Sickness In A brain disorder pay sickness in A Brain Danger pay sickness in A ILLness pay sickness in A brain ILLness brain danger sickness in a mental ILLness I'm getting paid for mental ILLness sickness tranzone JPS Hosital sickness ILLness Lawyers sickness mind 1023 Zillion dollar mental ILLness sickness north texas hostipal sickness middle wood clinic Oxygen sickness Tulane in Broad street evil old me 100 sill ion dollar with people evil dies died evil die Christ living Christ live Christ life good picture Book ass ho wrong evil wealth sinner under jail row underLaw Boxes 10,019 under jail time underLaw under born no born not born never born no born for gotten money not born with no money not born for gotten Sinner never born with out no money never born with not one sinner never born Mental ILLness froest never no not Born mental ILLness.

Keisha ann jacquet, kee-keedy Keisha jacquet me myself I see way out me myself I Keisha me myself I kee-kee me myself I keddy me myself lkee-keedy nicknames Kee nicknames Burkee nicknames

Burkeedy nicknames.

Mental ILLness weight, mental weight evil weight WXZ weight SOS weight Burden weight Burn weight False weight False Burden weight nigger weight disease weight Judgment weight Jealous weight lie weight Back Lie weight Burden Back Lie plot story weight Brain danger head weight brain danger Body weight brain tubes head weight brain tubes body weight evil enemies Christ height ABC height true story spirit Body height pound spirit height pound.

Keisha talk show Keisha talking show Keisha view show Keisha Real talk show Keisha view talk show Keisha view real talk show Keisha Beauty Keisha Beautiful Keisha glad Keisha green sea Keisha trust

Keisha happen Keisha happy Keisha Joyed Keisha supposed Keisha glad Keisha greensea Keisha yellow sea Keisha blue sea Keisha redsea Keisha Investments Keisha investigor, Keisha Delcago Community college 2001—2004 Keisha George Washington school Keisha federick A Douglass high school1997-2001 Keisha C.J. Colton Middles school1996-1997 Keisha music Art Keisha music show Keisha music CD Keisha DVD Keisha music technique Keisha art technique Keisha Lawyers Keisha Law suit Keisha judgments judge Keisha Doctor Keisha court house Keisha Washington D.C. Keisha white house Keisha legal boes Keisha legal Keisha legal police Boxes Keisha legal private privacy policy Keisha legal law suit Keisha legal lawyers negative Lawyers fake frost false not no real Lawyers evil light Christ Darkness evil A fear evil Keisha first time Keisha second time Keisha three time first time Love Keisha first Dairy time Keisha extra Love extra on Keisha extra Keisha Romaine Love.

Take me to the Queen l come to the Queen for prayers I can to the queen for praise. lean to the queen for prayers, I can to A Queen for blessing I can to a queen for tell a story lean to A Queen for a Beninning Rose is red violet or blue I love a green money I can to A Queen start I can to the queen for trust I can to A queen for trust I can to A Queen for trust lean to A Queen for faith take me to a queen take me to A Queen take me to the Queen take me to the loyal take me to A Loyal me myself I see way out.

GATES DEATH GATES DIE GATES DIED GATES DIES GATES DYES GATES ENEMIES Flood 13 gates died under written story under mistakes born under written born underlaw born died row born dies row born dyes row born die row born enemies under under mistakes underlaw under written inverstigor enemies investigor under law boy men enemies investigor scandal underlaw gates enemies underlaw scandal fake, false froest not no real at all nonfiction, non—faction out sides gates enemies sides line gates enemies underlaw gates enemies under mistake gates enemies underwritten gates enemies 12 gates Daughter queen gates 13 under written evil done under law evil gone.wxz jealous destroy evil sos died sentence enemies dyes charge enemies die sentence enemies die charge enemies death sentence enemies dearth charge enemies dead sentence enemies dead charge enemies wxz charge enemies wxz sentence enemies evil got that for gotten under law HIV Texas HPV Texas under law under written sex underwritten sex have STD disease Black moon red moon yellow moon Blue sky moon is the earth. Keisha under Law 42 people Back lie plot story Keisha under Law Booked story keep in touch ASAP/ P.S. thanks you

The story is about Base on fake story there are not real Base on a Jealouse Lie plot story A In heritance a inherit the hypocrite A increase A invisible A in no cents A inward the in grave A foolish A fool A foolishness the foot stool who is your enemies how can your enemies Be a Against you over something that on this story about base on a false story or not real who are your enemies what is your enemies were did your enemies take place at Keisha will you fix my life my self how many jealous people or how many people there have with Keisha Ann Jacquet. What kind jealous Do you have on Keisha they have jealous in the world with Keisha hating is out world in earth.

British accents a father is someone to reach out in have faith into him. Presidents Obama's is good he a nice dad. She going wow her bad behaved bad condition bad defective some man have evil disease catch worn for another people some catch Bacterium for boys in girl go get a check go see the doctor right a ways like disease another people like pussy in dick go see the scope. The father is my hero to me there is a hero went you face the world a long to reach you are there is affective influenced by or resulting from emotions affective Disorder by man baby dad and father.

Keisha think she after Birth Keisha got government federal and states by Law justice, judge, judgment my father have agree on me.

3 CHAPTER : KEISHA CAST OUT ENEMIES

My names is Keisha Ann Jacquet I'm going tell you mind story about myself this is nice picture or my drawing in the book a poem is a base true story I have people tell them about my book on face book in Lin kin .com I waiting on this life forever. In the past looked over my family generation of Christ true friend people around my house in the neighbor tell them my story some of I missing very much love to you. My story start on in 1982-2012 that it end this years to start over for the Beginning this year's 2012 it going to stive on the city people keep same the world going to end By fire the Red sea on the dark cloud around it. Some time the people make the end in the world to days much love to giving peace of mind in people don't let it go ways to be rejoiced over rainbow land with Berry fruit cake on what a sun set out sides just thanks about how your life turn around in up with people you can't could net I never through my family turn they back on me over my life in a book share over a salves person still take it off all the ways run they mouth on each other mouth thanks you for being there for me want I down in out no way around on it. Be the darkness shadow the wall floor. in the darkness people you cannot see better they white eye in the dark but the enemies will being me my light on the sky or Blue.

I don't worry about a little boy that can't could control me of what they have doing right now he tried to could control me but I'm jump off him right a ways over come him there air head tried to block fish ways or craft ways but the lord tell my one ears in my right go pay my due around the world obey him is commandments I try to make a vow to the lord in. I want turn back any more he touch my heart filling with goal everyday or the weak the lord said thank about yourself before of rose are red violet or blue looking over my life. I see straight people around me that is flesh in fear the globe around me. That is a poey for my Romans in judes shaken beer a story base on true make out gave so great full over my life Be then thanks for every thing's Rose is red violet or blue stop the crime I or violet take by force who is the force is the evil people that of afraid of water in talking about killer people fear of time by Black salves let my people go for free gang with violet to be stive back of enemies. Rose is red violet or blue let my rainbow come knee me right now. I see brother hood can get a long for each others like sister tried to stive in killer for each others peace be with you what you blind on this earth will not blind heaven strive in killer for each others peace. Blind eye fire red Blood run down sand he worries to be prayer poem story.

CHAPTER: KEISHA MUSIC STORY

What up cheatin, never win, in never win something always Happen to lose if you are a cheatin you never win as A lose something always happen to the end cheatin cheatin never win never something always happen to cheartin Birch. There is a hero looking inside your heart you don't have to be afraid what you are there is a answers inside A Heart. Wash the hatin off wash A nigger off me wash the jealous off wipe the niggers ho ass off me wipe the nigger ho off me can get an enough for me wipe the nigger off me wash the ho ass off me.

If you from the 9wards fuck ho ass if you from the New Orleans fuck ho if you from the 8 wards fuck ho if you from the Mississippi fuck ho if you from the 7 wards fuck ho you from the Texas fuck ho he. he are my husband I see is boost let make a family kids he are my niggers I see is ho out him let stop this crime let stop violet let stop a gang fright if you from the 6 wards fuck ho if you from the Atlanta Georgia if you from the Washington go hell if you from Florida go to hell I love you do you love me to. Wipe the hatin off me there are going straight to hell they need river flow Rhymes word make send cents Sinner don't make no cents rhymes word Sinner don't make any cents.